BEAUTIFUL CHANGELINGS

Also by Maxine Beneba Clarke

Foreign Soil

The Hate Race

Carrying the World

The Saturday Portraits

How Decent Folk Behave

For Children

The Patchwork Bike (illustrated by Van T Rudd)

Wide Big World (illustrated by Isobel Knowles)

Fashionista

Meet Taj at the Lighthouse (illustrated by Nicki Greenberg)

When We Say Black Lives Matter

Eleven Words for Love (written by Randa Abdel-Fattah)

It's the Sound of the Thing

Stuff I'm (Not) Sorry For

Praise for

MAXINE BENEBA CLARKE

'One of the most compelling voices in Australian poetry.' – *Overland*

'readers are left with the sense they have been seen, heard and understood' – *Books+Publishing*

'Maxine Beneba Clarke is a powerful and fearless storyteller.' – Dave Eggers, internationally bestselling author of *A Heartbreaking Work of Staggering Genius*

'deserves the widest possible audience' – *The Economist*

'a superb curation of uncomfortable truths' – *Mascara Literary Review*

'Maxine's writing is incendiary, insightful and hilarious' – *The Weekly Review*

'utterly compelling' – *Australian Financial Review*

'provides a voice and a ballast to the vulnerable, the sidelined and the forgotten' – *ArtsHub*

MAXINE BENEBA CLARKE

BEAUTIFUL CHANGELINGS

Published in 2025 by Ultimo Press,
an imprint of Hardie Grant Publishing

Ultimo Press
Gadigal Country
7, 45 Jones Street
Ultimo, NSW 2007
ultimopress.com.au

  ultimopress

A catalogue record for this book is available from the National Library of Australia

beautiful changelings
ISBN 978 1 76115 456 0 (paperback)

Cover design Allison Colpoys
Cover images Woman's face by Serge Filimonov / Stocksy; sea shells by Tatjana Zlatkovic / Stocksy; planet by Evan Dalen / Stocksy; model by Elena Kharichkina / Stocksy; scallop shell by Robert Winkler / iStock; mother of pearl sea shells by Natalia-flurno / iStock; blue and purple butterfly wings by Oleksii Kriachko / iStock; butterfly wing macro by Pansfun Images / Stocksy; woman's hand by Ivan Ozerov / Stocksy; pink dahlia by Kristin Duvall / Stocksy
Author photo Courtesy of Leah Jing McIntosh
Text design Simon Paterson, Bookhouse
Typesetting Bookhouse, Sydney | 12/16.6 pt Bembo MT Pro
Copyeditor Ali Lavau
Proofreader Elena Gomez

10 9 8 7 6 5 4 3 2 1

Printed in China by RR Donnelley.

MIX
Paper | Supporting responsible forestry
FSC® C144853

The paper this book is printed on is from FSC® certified forests and other controlled sources. FSC® promotes environmentally responsible, socially beneficial and economically viable management of the world's forest

Ultimo Press acknowledges the Traditional Owners of the Country on which we work, the Gadigal People of the Eora Nation and the Wurundjeri People of the Kulin Nation, and recognises their continuing connection to the land, waters and culture. We pay our respects to their Elders past and present.

For my mother,
and my children,
and for all who need it.

CONTENTS

PROLOGUE

incantation

let us bathe
in the sunset
before our twilight

let us bask
in the twilight
before our dusk

steady the song that,
tentative, trembles

breathe in, my sisters,

    and *believe*

BEAUTIFUL CHANGELINGS

beautiful changeling

you beautiful changeling, you:

golden, in the autumn
of your being

you hip-softness, you
white-wisped crown,
you tender-breast, you
gentle-step, you
other-worldly papering
of once-taut skin,
you fierce-wisdom, you

make-betterer
of scrapes, and
bad takes, and
playground squabbles,
          and world wars

you safety, you
home, you world

beautiful changeling

you sharp, you
unyielding

you *stuff being nice*, you
taking back my time,
you telling it like it is, you
not suffering fools

you *ungladly*

you *why don't you fucking fix it then*,
you filling the space, you
unleashing your tongue,
you *seen it all*

you holding their gaze, you
flaming their scorn

you unfettered power, you
        disturbingly carefree

you glorious,
uncomfortable joy

you enchanting
multiplicity, you
ancient mantra, you

starlight spell

you savage-unknowable,
you terrifying strength

you beautiful changeling, you
beautiful changeling,

go on

i want to grow old

i want to grow old

i want to grow old,
in a lime-green fake-fur coat
and oversized icon glasses

i want to be iris-apfel-fabulous,
i want to grow old-ungracious

i want to leave late-joan-didion impact,
but be dark joan-didion-elusive

let me grow old, let me
grow old, oh
let me grow old

i want to grow old
like toni morrison grew older:

regal, grey-majestic,
silver locks a tumbling sculpture

speaking slow, and exact,
and *only sense*
i want to grow old
like her

i want to grow old,
and not with tales of how:
when i was younger,
damn, i really was somebody
to be reckoned with

i want to be weighted
in my aunty era: with
post-generational knowledge
i want to grow old

i want to grow older
than womenfolk before me

to outlive my mother, who
outlived her mother,
who outlived her mother, who
outlived hers
but knowing
their kinship
led me here
so i could grow old, so
i could grow old,
so i could grow old

        with weathered hands
that braided hair,
took temperatures;
band-aided knees

but i'm gonna
        grow old

for me

in leather pants,
with a bright red walking stick,
in a neon plastic rocking chair,
slinging angela davis side eye
with a whiskied
          cup of tea

i want to grow so old
that i know in my bones
that it is time to leave

i want to grow old,
i want to grow old
          spectacularly,

and every evening
face tomorrow, knowing
          if it does not come,

i lived, and loved,

and with all i was given,
did the best i could

that i fought
for the world i wanted,
with as little harm
as i could manage

that i cooked,
and ate, and served up
          mostly good

i want to grow old
like lee lin, joan and toni:
old, in a lime-green fake-fur coat,
grow old, iconically

i want to grow old
with sex and scandal,
amongst darling friends,
with ferocity;

unashamed of how
this body wrinkles, bends
and creaks,

in reverence
of the fact
that here i am—
oh, here i am,
          grown *old*

just so you know

just so you know,
          i was cooler than you:
a sick hypercolour angel
with the puberty blues

i was slappin on my slap bands
bladin with no stackhat,
lolly gobble blissin
acid-wash tight jeans

kids, just so you know,
          i was hipper than you,
in my neon pink and yellow
parachute tracksuit; matchin
fingerless gloves, and a high fan fringe
van ice happy pants,
like an *ice, ice* dream

kids, just so you know,
i was *bad to the bone*,
bummin menthol durries
on my fifth chiko roll

chewin chewin gum yum
like young kylie mole,
she goes, she goes, she goes, she goes, she just—
kids, just so you know,
we were latchkey kids,
none-a this: *can we uber eats*
an afternoon treat

heads in the pantry
for a stale arrowroot,

or, if we struck luck,
a rad home brand noodle
(losers boil water,
had it dry from the packet)

we de-bratted brat
before the *summer of the brat*, it's

original gen,
and original x:
apathetic
just-let-it
get-it-done

no mess

flunked from degrassi
          and were born into punk;
forging dollarmite slips,
boom-shaked to the funk

kids, just so you know,
we rocked the mullet first:
white westie boys,
it was crimpin for the girls

black salt-n-pepa box braids,
flat tops, jheri curls:
collar wasn't greasy,
then your do wasn't *worth*

kids, just so you know,
yeah, just so you know
we go, we go, we go, we go—

we'll fuckin take teen spirit
to the nursin home

the change

they say
the change,

as if we have not always
been evolving:

for every new purpose,
and at every new turn

we, who are always
slick with new blood

shedding shape,
with the rounding
of the moon

hot flush debut

dark hours

my skin moves:
anemone, mucosal

peeled-back sheets

the damp and slick

my face, my back,
nape of the neck:

claggy to touch,

hot flush

the room a sauna,

gasping reach
for bedside water—

flush

my eyes roll back

i've stopped resisting

flush

cause fuck,
who doesn't like
a free hallucinogen
my god,

let's climb this sauna's
salmonella heat

arrhythmia,
a pulsing thunder:

blood-rushed,
beating at my temples

rasping air,
i scale the micro-fever

to the landscape of
surreal dreams

where tongue
becomes
an eagle's wing,

and every face
          is my face

throat ached open,
body dangling,

trapped in snarl
and sweat,

it's just too—

          flush

a laughing hall
of mirrors

then

sudden lucidity,
a clammy shiver:

every pore
a sober shock
of cold

i would like a hysterectomy

i

just ask them for it:

you might have years of this,
you're in pain, and really,
it's about your quality of life

your hormones indicate
you are nowhere near
menopause

besides, didn't a doctor there
offer you this option

once before

ii

in the quiet teal-toned
gyno clinic waiting room,
i replay the conversation
with my gp;

stare at the patterned carpet,
and practise, again,
        inside my head
i would like a hysterectomy, please
i would like a hysterectomy, please
i would like a hysterectomy, please

resolute,
like it's the only way
to return

        to kansas

iii

the doctor tries
        to lighten the mood
with several dad jokes,

but as much as i appreciate
his comedic efforts,

i am completely focused
on the task at hand

he runs me through
a familiar list of options

when he pauses,
at the end
of the surgery catalogue,

i take a deep breath,

and say my line

iv

back in the clinic waiting room,
i try to fill out the surgery form,

but i am so upset
my handwriting

is barely legible

okay, well,

if that's the option
you're most comfortable with,

let me run you
through the risks:

internal bleeding,
bowel perforation,
urinary or other incontinence,
early menopause, if for some reason
they can't keep your ovaries

and some women, well,
          they don't realise
how emotionally attached they are
to that part of their body

until their womb
is gone

i sign
    to have the fibroids cut out
by hysteroscopic myomectomy

maybe this is right, i tell myself,
after all, it is less risky, and

he's the professional

v

my surgery time
is eight-thirty
ante meridiem:

i am very early
on the day's list

early,
    after waiting
ten months,
haemorrhaging
two weeks a month

for a lesser operation

i fold my clothes;
order my belongings

with way too much care
          and precision,

in consideration

of whoever may need
to collect them

if, perchance, this
scratchy cotton gown
is the last thing
    i end up wearing

i am weighed

they take my blood, absurdly,
          to check for pregnancy

they ask,
for about the tenth time, if i am

done with having kids

vi

in the waiting area,
they hand out blankets

sitting all in a row,
in our matching uniforms,
it feels like a prison admission

the smiling nurse hands out
five tiny transparent cups

with a pill in each of them

the other women down them

and i wonder,
    if i've somehow missed
the explanation

excuse me,
        i call the nurse over

        it's to dilate your cervix

i nod,
as if i, too,
now understand,
    and i take the medication

vii

the woman next to me,
    twenty years my senior,
has thinning dark hair,

a thunderous laugh, a
try-me vibe

feels like being her friend
          would be an absolute riot

she tells me it's not menopause
that's the problem:
it's how capitalism
refuses to adapt
to the nature
     of some women's bodies

when the flushes got real bad,
she got jack of no one understanding

and quit

no way she was working
through that everyday hell so
          some already-rich bastard

could accumulate
more generational wealth

she doesn't own much herself,

not even her home,

but it's only her,
and the two cats,

and now,

she watches netflix
through the flushes,
and catches up on sleep
in the afternoons

i think, *god, this makes so much sense*
i think, *i would like a hysterectomy*

i think, *when i grow up, i want to be you*

viii

an impossibly nonchalant man,
with an official black clipboard,
wanders in

    to where we're all sitting

white coat over casual clothes,

        seems too young
to be the surgeon

he sits down next to me,
and explains,
        in an english accent
so laddish it startles me

        he's a medical researcher,
observing how women
respond to anaesthesia

will i give him permission
to watch my surgery

nothing will change

he won't participate, he'll

    just observe

i'm kind of stunned

to him, i am cells,
tumour, and tissue

but a six-foot-tall,
grown white man
is smiling, *next to*

a black women he has
never met before, asking

can i watch,

while you lie unconscious,
and they access your uterus
through your cervix

to cut your fibroids out

and i don't know,
it just seems
like there should be

a better
fucking
protocol

he reminds me *it's for medical research,*

he tells me *personal information*
will be de-identified

i look around

i am the only
black woman here

is race a de-identified characteristic

the consent form he offers
          is seven pages long,

i don't have the time,
am not in the frame of mind,
to make sense of it

i think, *henrietta lacks*
i think, *anarcha*

i think, *dr marion sims*
i think, *the tuskegee experiment*

i think of all the times
i've written about this
    same old disrespectful shit

i think of the doctor
who sent me here,

i think,

i would like a fucking hysterectomy

NO!

the room
falls deathly quiet

the other patients sign:
every single one of them

a tattooed young woman,
impossible asymmetrical cut
carved into fawn hair,

says: *of course you can observe*

and thank you,
you and your team,

for all you do for
women's health

as she speaks,
she gives me

a what-the-fuck-is-wrong-with-you
          side eye

which, to be honest,
just seems

unnecessarily
spiteful

ix

i am cramping
like my abdomen
    is trying to get away from itself

i tell a nurse

she brings me

a disposable
hot-water pack

i have been waiting
three hours now

the woman who's a riot,
the asymmetrical haircut
and the others

who came in after me

have been called

        into surgery

i mention this
to a third nurse
        who's sitting at the counter,
drinking steaming hot tea

she tells me
there are lot of operating theatres
they each have their own schedule

could be there's an emergency in yours

i would like a hysterectomy,

        or at the very least
the surgery they have

prepped me for

x

well past midday
a young female doctor
ushers me into a private room

she looks uncomfortable,

like she was specifically selected
to soften bad news

she tells me:

the morning surgery spots
have all been taken up

they'll have to schedule me
          for another day now

i say, *my surgery time was eight-thirty am*
i say, *i've been on the waiting list for ten months*
i say, *i've been here waiting for four and a half hours*
i say, *i've done the fasting*
i say, *my partner took time off work*
i say, *i had to get care for one of my children*

i think, *is this because i refused*
to let that random man
watch my surgery

i wonder how they decided

it would be me

i say, *i'm cramping*, i say,
they gave me something,
i ask, *am i going to be okay,*
if i go home?

the doctor smiles,
like i'm insane

for even asking

that should wear off
within the hour

she offers me a box of tissues

i'm so sorry,
sometimes this just happens

i leave the tissues where they are,
and wipe my eyes

with the back of my hand

xi

it doesn't
wear off within the hour,
that cramping

my body contorts,
as if it's possessed

i tell my partner,
i know what this is

i tell my partner,
i'm in labour

even though

both of us know
that's impossible

i call the nurse desk
and tell them,

i am having
what feels like
contractions

i ask the name
of the medication
            they gave me

we look it up

it is alternatively known as
the abortion pill

xii

the emergency nurses seem
like they don't believe my story

then they look me up
on the system,

and see that it's true

oh wow, they did—
they just . . . cancelled you

exchanging glances, like:
what the actual fuck
is this hospital

they tell me: *usually the effects are masked*
by the anaesthetic
          they use for the operation

i say, *i was never told what they gave me,*
and i was given no discharge information

they immediately temper
their outrage,

after all, they
    are part of the machine

i think about the women
who went in before me

and how they might never know
they took this thing

good for them, i think,
good for goddamn them

xiii

they cannot reverse
the effects of the drug

but they can give me endone
until it wears off

the endone
makes a purple genie
          of my rage

the purple endone rage-genie
shrouds itself dramatically
    in smoke

the purple endone rage-genie
says i have three wishes,
before he gets
          his freedom

we drive back home

with the purple endone rage-genie
lazing across the backseat

the genie asks,

do i need a moment
do i need a moment

to think about my three wishes

i say, *i don't need a moment,*
purple endone rage-genie,
i am absolutely sure

i say, *i would like a hysterectomy*
i would like a hysterectomy
i would like a hysterectomy

the genie

unrolls a long train
of yellowed parchment,

and starts
    to read me

the risks

xiv

two weeks later,
back in the surgery rooms,

i tell them:

i am not having a pregnancy test,
will not be weighed, or
take any medication before surgery
i am first on the list today, and i will kick up merry hell
        if you try to bump me

the check-in nurse

slowly reads the file notes

she says,

i don't know
if we can do all that for you

but i hold strong,

and eventually,

        they do

xv

three days after surgery
i am still bleeding

i bleed as easily as i'm breathing, blood
soaks through the maxi-pads, my undies
and my jeans

the nurses at emergency
are old friends now:

we've been through shit

once again,
they *can't believe it*

they keep me in for a couple hours
until a doctor can do *the internal*
then send us home,
to wait it out

xvi

three bleeding days later,
i am back,

and this time,
i can barely stand

they stick little
round resuscitator stickers

all over my chest

xvii

finally, someone
checks the surgery notes

oh, this explains it,

the new emergency doctor says,

one of the fibroids
was embedded
in your uterus

so they just took off
what they could

they probably expected
it to clot

i lie dizzy, under
the fluorescent lights

thinking, *i would like a hysterectomy,*
thinking, *you could not make this up*, thinking:

the surgeon
cut a fibroid
in half,

    and just

never
thought
to
fucking
mention it

a tranexamic acid drip later,

i leave, with three weeks' worth of
anti-bleeding medication
and hormones:

eighteen tablets a day

and after twenty-one days,
if you stop the medication
and the bleeding comes back,

then just go back on it

indefinitely,

we'll check in with you
at your clinic visit,

if you're not happy
with how things are going,

unfortunately,

we might have to talk

about a hysterectomy

i think, *i do not want a hysterectomy*

i think, *no matter what happens next,*
one thing is for sure:

you folks here

will not
be touching me

xviii

when things settle down,
i insist on an ultrasound

i want to know

how badly

        they have scarred
the wall of my uterus

that's so weird, says
the sonographer,

the initial report
says you have adenomyosis,
as well as the fibroids

i'm very surprised,

very surprised
that the doctor
    recommended

you have
that kind
    of surgery

how much, this weight

the weight
        of existing

as a black poet,
and a black mother, and
a black woman, and
before that, a black, black girl
in a white-world reckoning, and

how much of this weight i'm carrying
was genetically engineered
by slavery's black-mammying

engineered to keep me soft,

and caring for anyone
who wants to land

for sex, or food,
free labour

                comfort

or whatever else

they need,

or whatever else

        they can take
from me

how much, this weight
i'm carrying, how much,

how much of this weight
i carry is a bloodline forced
to farm the food bowl
of a stolen world

but never let
to grow the seeds
they secreted, precious,
    from home

never allowed
the language
of our own

the tongue, you see,
is colonised

in far more ways
        than one

how much, this yam-less bread,
this babe-less breast, this
insatiable hunger, this

weight

this weight

how much, this weight

        i'm carrying

the body keeps song

i

bare them, my friend
they are made of wonder:

the deflated wing casings
beneath the upper arms

show them, in the sunlight:
your brachii, sunken

the soft, spent
        magic
that sings
of your grace

ii

fingers, hidden in dishwater,
laundry, soil, and shame

crooked-undainty,
both yours, and mine

let's unglove them
at dinner,

without a care

at pudding, we'll splay them
in sheer delight

and cast off shame,
at this arthritic crumpling

marvelling
          at how
we've held
this life

iii

your veins, a map
of the journeys
and detours:

a delicate, spidering
varicose bloom

tracing rivers
          and plains
since you passed
the meridian

how wondrous
you made it here,
my friend

iv

scattered,
          like dappled light:
on hips, thighs, arms:

a glittering

saying this is where
i stretched, and changed,
and grew
          past

merely *fitting*

VOCATIONAL SCHOOL FOR GIRLS

the *when* vows

the *when* vows

are proclaimed in cobwebbed cubbyhouses;
whispered under the big red slide

passed nonchalantly along imperfect pliés,
in the grade one ballet class

when i get married, and
when i have babies,
when i meet my husband,

at my wedding

girls, echoing
          back at us
the expectations of the world

when i'm ceo,
when i'm happily single,
when i've bought that house
          for myself

when i get my degree,
or *when i write my first book,*
or *when i tell my boss to get fucked*

when i am the boss,
when i am 'that bitch'

when i'm in parliament,
when i storm the world

when my album goes platinum,
when i've helped cure cancer,
when i'm number-one heavyweight,
and all

when i swim with the sharks,
as i run with the wolves

once i'm fighting climate change, for sure

when i'm whatever kind of person
i was born to be:

my very soul singing,
and free

when i've completely destroyed
the heteronormative
white supremacist

patriarchy

the boy diet

several years
after i was born,
my mum and her friend

went on *the boy diet*

p&c committee gossip had it

    if you followed
this particular eating plan,

you were guaranteed
to conceive

a beautiful
baby boy

mum can't remember
    what she ate

(when i ask, she laughs:
i don't know . . . but it was
probably ridiculous)

about a year later,
each of them gave birth
to the sons
their husbands wanted

she concedes
the diet had little to do with it

but adds, *yet, somehow,*
it worked!

i am the second daughter:
a father's disappointment,

and the joy
of an unbothered woman

who ate exactly
what she
        wanted

test match

my fifth grade crush
was rad at sports;

had kind, hazel eyes
        and knobbly knees
lined with the faint white scars
of myriad soccer injuries

a white bread
and margarine boy

with a long-fringed bowl cut
    he'd had since preschool,
    back in 1983

a smattering of honey-coloured freckles
fell so prettily
        across his nose
they looked drawn on
with eyebrow pencil

lewis
        leaned across my desk,
one friday afternoon,

to speak to his friend
are you going to cricket practice
this afternoon?

i knew little about cricket,
except it was definitely boring

where do you play?
i asked, casually as i could,
imagining myself
happening to walk past, just
so i could see him outside of school

sunnyholt road,
snapped his friend,
but you can't join our team,
because we don't allow girls

we don't allow girls

we don't allow girls,
and i forgot
about my crush

we don't allow girls,
i thought, *rightio,*
we'll see about that then

the next morning,
over orange marmalade toast,
mum said
    i never knew
    you liked cricket

i squirmed, under
her suspicious stare,

    i do, but they
    don't allow girls

that's all i said,
they don't allow girls,
and mum forgot

that i didn't like cricket

next friday practice, there i was
(the coach entirely unhappy about it):
the bolshie black girl,
with the powder-puff pony,

who'd infiltrated cricket club

escorted to the nets,
to show what i had,
(i didn't even know
how to hold a bat)

i swung,
          to no avail

the boys all groaned,
and swore under their breath:

          their championship
slipping through the nets

three practices later,
i got bored
and dropped out

sorry, turns out
cricket's just
not her thing

the team jeered, and
high-fived, and flopped
down on the pitch

but i walked away
a champion

vocational school for black girls

old-school, in
billowy blouses
and pearl earrings,

our mid-nineties
careers adviser

was consistently apathetic:

keening towards
a well-earned retirement

in our first meeting,
as my eyes wandered
over inspirational wall quotes,

she scrawled down

a list of traits

apparently gleaned
from our brief
conversation

two weeks later,
rubik's cube on her desk
betraying three half-peeled stickers,

she handed me
          my fortune

a piece of paper
that said:

nursing aide
childcare worker
nurse

she had my grades
printed out on her desk:
a straight-A student,
with a head for humanities

i stood to leave, and read,
upside down,

in her notebook

maxine,
the black girl,

best suited to
a service job:
care industry

ironing

i

sometimes, our family
hosted important guests:

visiting academics,
care of the mathematics faculty
where my father worked

except for the food,
we kids found it tedious

my third-trimester mother
        checked the roast chicken,
and sliced kiwifruit
for the pavlova

to everyone's surprise, our
well-mannered guest

had brought a present
for the tiny daughters:

wrapped in purple paper,
and excitingly large,

it was the only thing
my sister and i saw

we tore through tissue paper
with great gusto

squealing loudly in delight

behold:

a little ironing board,
and a teeny tiny toy iron

the way my mother tells it,

the lounge room turned quiet,

she could sense
          the gathering
of my father's rage:

he would not have

any of his daughters

playing at
keeping house

ii

i arrived on foot,
pushing a pram,

the owner whispered
a polite
          hello

the apartment
was not ideal,

but nor was my situation,
          to be totally real

the colour scheme
was a fever dream
of deep burgundy carpet
and bright blue walls

we stepped out
into the mould-mottled courtyard,
and mosquitoes clouded, like smoke

          do you have any questions,
she asked hurriedly

the washing machine
fixings were in the bathroom

i don't think so,

then, just to be polite

is there anything
you want
to ask me?

she cleared her throat
and, nervously,
shifted weight to the other foot

do you own an iron?

i laughed, said no,
emphatically,

good:
the last tenants
pressed their clothes
on the floor

the owner let out
a sigh of relief,

they left scorch marks, seared
into the brand new carpet,

but you don't own one, do you

iii

twelve dollar fifty
k-catalogue special:

the first iron
i've owned in a decade

and a half

bought to fasten labels
onto prep school uniforms,

and never used again

so when my eldest stumbles,
creased, from his room,
asking
        do we own
        one of those . . . things?

i screw up my face, and
point him to the chaos
beneath the kitchen sink

behind pots and shopping bags,
unused candles,

and the general debris
        of living

prettier

her, honey-haired
from grandparent's dutch blood,

hailing from the country:
grenfell, to be exact

me, the diaspora black girl
from the white edge
of the western 'burbs

but it worked

meaning, as undergrads
we found we could live
with each other, literally

we met in creative writing class:
the only two in a double degree with law,

but she'd transferred to law-commerce
very soon after writing semester started

we poets were too rambling
and bohemian for her

i liked that:
we were all fumbling, out there,
but she knew, already,
what was not her jam

saturday mornings,
there was always
some boyfriend of hers
          in our kitchen
(they were mostly quite lovely,
except for that one)

and between work, and classes,
and the uni bar, and classes, we'd talk,
as young friends are prone to do

about our families back home,
and our upbringings, and
how we were going
          to *really live*

she knew about my sister:
the star student athlete,
who'd had a good run
in modelling comps
when we were younger

one afternoon,
she walked into my room
to borrow something,
and saw a sibling photo
tucked
          into the corner
of a picture frame on my wall

she plucked it from its perch,
sat down on my unmade bed

a minute passed,

then she said,
surprise lacing her voice:

you know, your sister is taller,
and thinner, and all that—
but on the bones of it,
you're prettier than her

it was one of those moments
that destroy your world

i hated how good
those words made me feel

THE SIRENS

the sirens

they reclined,
        bare-breasted, atop the cliffs
pulling shell comb
through thick, dark hair;

preening, drinking
the sirenuse sun,

wings ruffled
by the gentle
        sea breeze

few enraptured
by their arias,
lived to describe them

those who did
were never
        the same

when you have heard

the hum of the heavens,

how do you,
    mortal,
go on

sailors, distracted,
craned their necks,

and captains, overcome,
    would tilt:

and manoeuvre
their lurching vessels around:
enchanted, and sobbing
    at the helm

days later,

weary islanders

would haul the corpses
from shallows and weed

of bruised,
rigor-mortis-smiled,
salt-bloated men

who could not keep
    their gaze

to themselves

autonomy

in the beginning,
god made adam and eve,

and eve's complete,
and unfettered,

autonomy

devil in her ear,
          or not,
the very first woman
was divinely designed,

to do whatever
the fuck

she wanted

boxing day

boxing day
comes quiet:
a child was born
in bethlehem,
beneath a star,

but a childhood died

'wise men' brought
frankincense and myrrh,

for a boy
who had not
opened his eyes,

but did they gather
that young girl in their arms
and whisper
oh, sweet darling,
it's okay to cry,
you are not alone tonight

a scared child
carried a god's fire
in her belly
without a choice;

saw a young man
she birthed
and raised

murdered on a cross,
crowned in thorns

on boxing day,

    i think
    about mary

men who made of us monsters

we, the demon-jealous,
who poisoned our own;

trapped daughters
in the sunless cellars

we, who flung stepchildren,
barefoot and afraid,
into the dark, dark woods

we built houses of candy:
spun sugar traps,

conjured towers;
polished arsenic apples

we, who stole the ocean's
        most stunning of voices;

hurled bewitchings,
and all manner of curse

we, who made sure
that beauty
          was put to sleep

we, the liars:
unhinged, and vengeful

oh, we were so rendered
by the fictions of men

it was *their ink*,
that made of us

          monsters

spindle

flour embedded
in the crisscross
of my cornrows;

fingers softening
shortcrust dough,

and every cracking joint
a reckoning

the chef, pacing
the production line,
muttering:
 every element
 must be fit
 for a king

the air, tart
with green apple, and
sweet with cinnamon,
and spiced with the fire
of ginger skin

in the palace kitchen,
where i worked,

the rule was:

only one sharp knife
per shift

one of beauty's parents
—the king, or the queen—
would sit in the corner,
          and watch

as we passed
the offending utensil
down the line,

slicing figs, and
peeling potatoes,
and scaling fish

we'd wash the blade

in a bowl of soapy water
                    in between

never the knife
would slip
from their sight

it was the same
with anything sharp:

the woodcutter's axes,
the tailor's darning needles,
the governess's sharpener,
and the gardener's shears

nobody knew,
well, not for sure,

why pointy
          or jagged
things

were not permitted
on the palace grounds

but believe you me,
we talked

beauty's nurse
said something to me
once

she said:

everyone assumes
it's easy
to be a princess,

but sometimes,
that young girl
disappears
into the bathroom,

and emerges
with her face
salt-streaked from tears

nurse went
to the king
about it

king
    stuck an afro-pick
in his curly black mane,

and said his daughter was
just growing up:

you know how emotional
women can be

he told beauty's nurse
some complicated tale

about an angry aunt-in-law

from that voodoo island
just off the coast

of dutch-colonised
sint maarten:

he said aunty got angry,

because she wasn't invited
to beauty's christening

    apparently
    she was always
    so troublesome,

she flew in anyway,

and for her grand-niece's gift,
well, she cursed that tiny babe

beauty wouldn't die *immediately*,
but definitely by the time
she turned sixteen:

she'd prick her finger
on something sharp,

a spinning wheel, perhaps,

and well, *that would be it*,
beauty: *dead*

the royals thrown into
an eternity of grief

the king claimed that it was all
just in case, the no-blades rule—
that he didn't really believe it,

but that man searched the kingdom:
had all the spinning wheels
smashed to pieces

cause you can never
be too careful
now, can you

nurse thought
the king'd been drinking
(he often talked nonsense,
after a goblet or two)

so in the end, as far as beauty
was concerned,
the staff consensus was:

we went knifeless in the kitchen
because the princess was depressed

on beauty's sixteenth birthday,
i carried the steaming apple pie
    (her favourite)
into a packed room, full
of people who loved her,
    (this time, not an aunty in sight)

it had taken just shy of four hours
to bake and decorate the thing

beauty happily blew the candles,
graceful as she ever was;
cut that first slice
with the side of
a serving spoon,

declaring:

i'd give my queendom
for a knife around here!

the guests,
and we servants,

we laughed,
and laughed,
and laughed

after all

here beauty stood:
sixteen, and alive,

and seeming jolly,
on this auspicious occasion,
    at least

beauty: finally safe

but late that afternoon,
as we were cleaning the kitchen,
beauty's limp body
was brought up
    from the basement:
a droplet of blood
still beading on her finger

she had somehow stumbled
upon a spindle

and now, was unresponsive

they sent three horsemen
for *the good aunt* then,

the one that knows those incantations

the good aunt arrived dishevelled:
        wiping pumpkin pie
from the corner of her mouth,
like she'd been summoned
        halfway through a meal

i was taking off my apron,

all ready to fetch my henry
from the fields,
so's we could go home,
via getting the children from mum's,

when they gently laid
    beauty's dead body
on the kitchen table

the king's voice thundered

nobody is to leave
you hear me?

no one is going anywhere!

we all just thought
they didn't want word
getting out
just yet

the aunt was muttering;
walking eerie circles
around her great-niece

she ummed, and uhhhed,
cracking her fingers, and
shaking her locs;

sucking her teeth

as fortune would have it,
i can't undo this, she finally said,
the most i can do is lessen it

from death,

to darkness
for one hundred years

king, queen and aunty
conferred
    in the corridor,
then his majesty boomed, forlorn,

if beauty must sleep,
then so must we all!

the nerve of that family—

as if we had no lives
outside their home

oh, the sweat on my palms,
the terrified catch in my throat,
and my god, the terror that rose

i turned my head,
          and through the kitchen window,
saw my henry, with that low amble of his,
approaching the castle

henry took in:
    the fear on my face,
the aunty's spirit-dancing,
lifeless beauty on the kitchen table

we locked eyes
          and i mouthed—

i mouthed *go! get out!*
i mouthed *i love you!*
and *look after the children!*

and henry turned,

henry turned, and ran:

he ran back across the gardens,
to the edge of the palace grounds,

then,

the ripple of my love's
workhorse shoulders; his unkempt curls
disappearing, as he quickly
    scaled the sandstone fence

and emerald leaves—

i saw emerald leaves, creeping
fast, towards me,

        as vines of allamanda snaked
around the window shutters

so nah, don't tell me—
don't tell *me*

        about the miracle
of that spoiled girl, waking,
finally, in the woods

because when darkness lifted,

i had lost everything:

henry, and my mother, and the kids:
the only life i knew

beauty should have died that day

and instead,

we, the servants,
          were locked in

there once was a woman

a nursery rhyme rewrite

there once was a woman
who lived in a shoe

she had so many children,
but knew what to do

they were clothed, fed,
loved and public schooled:

in a happy home,
a rambunctious brood

whispers had it she beat them,
after dry bread:

but most likely,
some hater had that spread,

and she was just *a good woman*
in a difficult situation,

whispered about all over town,
          but nonetheless,

trying her best

peter, peter, pumpkin eater

a nursery rhyme rewrite

peter, peter, pumpkin eater,
had a wife, and would not keep her

from the career
she'd nurtured for many years
old mate pete stayed home,
and looked after their kids

peter, peter, pumpkin eater,
had a wife, and would not keep her
but peter, peter was not bothered
pete and his wife, *they kept each other*

WOMEN'S WORK

hickory dickory dock

some nights,
        the urgent notes for poems
sat piled haphazardly
on the plywood desk
in my room,

and, twitching to have at them,

i'd wind
the giant analogue clock

on the far wall
        of the kitchen

with the orange scent
of a school day afternoon
        still hanging
beneath the clouds,

and the other children of the street
still playing tiggy
                outside,

i'd smile, and say, *genuinely* surprised:
          wow, would you look at the time
okay, kids, here's your dinner, and then,
time to get ready for bed

voice even, and easy

so they'd never cotton on
to the duplicity
          i'd set ticking

four pm, and there i'd be,
claiming, pan-faced
it was already six,
          in a series of performances
well worthy
of the academy

oh, they found out eventually, the kids

when their uncle
gave them an ipad

for christmas,

and with it,

a digital reference point

they thought it was
a riot,

and by then,

well,

by then
i'd birthed

collections

women's work

and just like that

we were stopping boardroom meetings
to hold recess breaks and unpeel cheese sticks

running *wiggles* on repeat
remembering to mute our zoom calls
when the toddlers wandered in

the pandemic
became *women's work*

our studios and offices
were kitchen tables

we made spreadsheets
next to fruit bowls, in the gaps between
our ten-year-old's new spelling list
and running twelve times tables

while the men made offices
of vacant sunrooms, moved

their plants in; hung *do not disturbs*
on doorknobs and lamented
how, bereft, the children,
missing little playmates, *made such noise*

soothing them was
women's work

just like that,
we lost the things
our mothers marched for
so we'd never have
to become them

some lost the things
we wore like crowns
(we are no less a woman,
or a mother, cause the things
that sing our souls,
    are made of more
than just the kids)

giving up

that job you can't sustain:
who'll manage the household dear,
we need my income, it's just logical

the pandemic
became women's work

though most the epidemiologists
and statisticians, most the
analysts and politicians
on the late-night news
    were men
(their colleagues
had other things to do)

women

sweeping up the nursing homes,
the childcare centres,
the debris of all our broken lives

women, sweeping up three times a day,
cause homes aren't really made to live in

not like this

with a resolve
            that leaves
the floorboards crumbed and sticky

women's work
was spinning dinner
out of nothing

women tended broken walls
marked with the fists of men, whose anger
and frustration at the world

was women's work

and in the centres,
women took the urgent calls of
other women just like them

women's work was
shrinking ourselves smaller
so we fit our shrinking worlds

so we eased the overcrowding

women's work was
trying not to take up too much space,
make too much noise

was knowing little ones
can't understand the distancing,
and always run to nanna
or their mama first

cause women's work
was standing in between

the virus and the children
in between the virus and our charges
in between the virus and our students
in between the virus and our partners
in between the virus and our elders
in between the virus and our patients

in between the virus
and our hearts

staffing schools in higher numbers,
shepherding unvaccinated youngsters;
washing down infected elders, and exhausted

charged with calming anxious minds

women, teaching classes
with their own kids round their ankles

women's work was nursing twelve-hour shifts
in masks so tight and long
that the elastic broke the skin

they say that *women hold up half the sky,*
but they don't say *the half they hold up's heavier*

and if you're sovereign on this land,

and if you're woman and you're black,
disabled, of a certain age,
alone, in charge of kids,
not cis, or woman and you're queer . . .

some women *always* knew,
but for the others

the pandemic showed us how,
even as women saved the world,
saving the world
    was women's work

a good wait

love a good time-wasting trip in the car:
kid has lost their transport card,
i'll just drive them, *door to door,*
honestly, really, *that's what i'm for*

not quite finished a dinner at their bestie's,
or *she's braiding my hair, and she can't leave the rest,*
i'll just idle in the driveway, *whatever, no problem,*
i'll recline the seat and *chill out* till they come, cause

i love a good time-wasting wait in the car:
in the heat of summer, when the aircon's struggling,
and if you crank it up parked, you'll max the battery,
love a good lean on burning duco, that's me

rehearsals run over for the school production,
and dinner's in the oven, on timer, back home;
theatre kid's texting: *mum! we have to run this scene!*
fucking bastion of fucking understanding, that's me

bloody love a good wait, love a wait in the car,
love a wet day pick-up when the friends pile in,
and the rain's horizontal, and you can't see the road:
block by insurance claim, dropping teens home

fucking love a group pick-up, pile them all in the back,
i'm such a zen driver: unstressed and relaxed,
who cares about the work zoom i should be doing,
when i can mum-taxi for whoever's kid's going

fucking love a good car pool, i love a good wait,
love a good school pick-up two-thirds through my day,
it's not hard to be patient, when waiting's your favourite,
just sitting in my vehicle, admiring the way

the minutes tick by, if it makes their lives better
i'll just wait outside till they're ready, forever,
bloody love a good wait, love a wait in the car,
love a car with a wait, and a wait in a car

love an idle in the driveway,
love a taxi-run wet day,
love a not-ready text, ay
no problem, i'll wait

hey mum, what's for dinner?

what's for dinner?

what's for ?
mum ?

what's ?
what's for dinner?

mum,
mum,
mum,
what's for dinner?
what's for dinner?
what's for dinner?
what ?
what ?
mum ?
mum ?
mum ?

acrostic

on the second sunday
of every may,

little kids go acrostic
all over the place

with:

marvellous
understanding
mum

forgetting what they wrote
        just twelve months earlier;

presenting their efforts
with their chests puffed out

and every may, on
the second sunday,
we close our cards,
chuffed, and smiling away,

saying: *wow,* that's
such a beautiful poem

you kids
          really

     made my day

american mum

a shadow poem

less than 24 hours

every so often,
we eye each other:
but what if we didn't, huh

the women of iceland
managed it once,

went all *lysistrata*:

refused to cook, and clean,
and coddle, and cuddle;
work-kowtow,
fetch-carry,

            and fuck

way back when,
in the seventies

i heard they brought
their country

to its knees

in less
than
24 hours

the day we fled

and get this,
we old women just left them there:
like the wiry hairs on our chins,
like the laugh lines from knowing
this thing was coming;
with our petrol gauges on full

we left dirty dishes in the sink, and
missed calls from our grown-up sons, saying:
mum, could you watch the kids tonight please,
we've both got something on

we left underwear
on the bathroom floor,
and we drained the bank accounts

it wasn't supposed to go this far,

but once we felt freedom,

we ran

possum magic

for claudette clarke

i

rummaging in the garage storage,
for some lost or other thing

i must've been, say,
        fourteen,

and that cardboard box,
        in particular

—thin layer of dust;
    top carefully tucked—

seemed
to be calling

curious rummaging
revealed a scrapbook,
which revealed
        a scattering
of news clippings:

pastings of my mother,

performing in a theatre in london;
guest-starring on a well-known
english soap, and—

i'd seen her on stage
a few times before,

we'd run lines
          in the living room
for *the crucible*,
and *to kill a mockingbird*

our whole family
had sat in the audience
at the ensemble theatre,

but—

after flipping through

the remainder of the blank pages
i brought the scrapbook to my mother,
    and asked

if she missed *doing more of this*;
why she'd given it up,

like, as an actual profession, i mean

she smiled,

and stared back lovingly

at one-quarter
        of the reason

ii

ushered to the best seats
in the house,

my children and i,

amidst the myriad rustlings
of programs, popcorn boxes,
gentle parental reprimands

        shuffling anticipation

the lights came up
on the darling quarter,

and there mum stood:

pointy ears at alert,
furry paws poised,
        and a painted purple apron
full of stars, and dreams

a collective gasp
from hundreds
        of small children,

and a round of applause
from their grown-ups:

as if suddenly, they'd remembered
    the child inside,
and therefore,

exactly who they were

it's grandma poss!

yelled a boy
in the front row

and the whole
enchanted theatre

hushed,

    and leaned in,

eager for the story
to begin

how fitting, to share
her magic

with the children
of this place

behold,

how stunning

her twilight is

MAJOR COMPLICATIONS

marionette

they choose the kind
who'd never march

see her dance:

a marionette,
across the newly polished
plate glass floor

swear her in

let's watch her

sacrifice

our daughters

major complication

a jazz poem

i

in 1955, a white woman
saw a black boy
in the mississippi grocery store
her family owned

that proved to be
a major complication

maybe he smiled too much,

was too happy,
too handsome,
or, for a black boy,
too goddamn smart
and self-assured

whatever the case
the upset of him
loomed large,
a complication in b major

and whatever small joy
carolyn bryant witnessed
emmett till eking out of life

took up residence
inside her head

so carolyn said

that boy looked at me

he whistled, brushed against my arm,
(whatever, in god's name,
that woman dreamed up)

she knew

her words
were packed with gunpowder,

and she did not give a fuck

emmett till was nothing but
a complication

someone's child
to hang from the hickory

that's exactly what
her intention was

emmett

till's

body

that's a pretty big
complication

emmett till,

and all the other black men,
and all the other black boys,
and all the other black folk,

they are imprints on our selves

black women, we are born
having seen that photo:

his blood
runs in ours,

no matter where we are born
in the world,
diaspora-black

emmett till, who in truth,
looked no more than twelve

a dear, sweet, baby-faced kid

bullet-ridden, swollen with river water,

flesh pocked, in the places
he'd been tortured

it
was
so
bad

the papers
ran the portrait

nothing but
a complication:

the all white jury
acquitted all white men
just like all white carolyn bryant
knew they all white would

here's his photo,
take a look:
sister, look real close
and look real good,

this is not
a minor complication:

a black child lying dead
cz a bored white woman

pointed

it is
an ongoing complication
to what you say you want:

the unconditional
sisterhood

ii

a complication

to what you say you want

cz *dark* are the daughters
yea, dark are the daughters
of the witch who did not burn

salem started

when two pre-teen white girls
    fashioned witching sticks,

and pointed them at tituba,
tituba, who'd loved them
most their lives

    a complication,
    a complication in b major

tituba was trying to save them
from a fever, with her herbs

cz she knew about
that kind of medicine, tituba,

it was a knowledge of her kin

she was sharing
with those white folk
her stalk, and leaf, and poultice; her
boiled bush tonic, heady and thick
with how brownwomenfolk like her
          used the very earth to heal

fetching and carrying
for that family
all the days
she could remember, tituba,

and there she was:
trying to heal their babies
with what she did not have to share

and just look—
just *look* at what she got

          the complication
for all that care

for edging those girls
from the fever
          burning at their brow

the reverend's daughters
started slinging mud,

mud they knew
would surely stick,

hurled,
          at the very woman
who raised them up,

(though the babies
she herself had borne
          were sent down river)

and this is what she got; this is
what they made sure they gave her,
that's right:

          a complication

dark are we,
the daughters
of the witch
who would not burn

cz tituba
          started pointing back
saying *she*, and *she* and *she*
and *she*

and i saw that white lady over there,
doing white magic, in the white woods
by the white light of the white moon

i saw she, and she, and she

take us to the forest edge
and light the match,
and we brown women
          will be made of wrath

tituba made sure
they got
          the complication

they were searching for

cz in the end, the whole of salem
smoked with death

wronged brown women, nah,
we don't mess around none

she gave them
a complication

and tituba, the original
victim of original witching,

she walked away unharmed

but
the major complication
stands:

that, well, salem only smouldered
because two white girls
made stick wands,

and accused
the *coloured* help

so we say *dark* are the daughters
yea, *dark* are the daughters

dark are the daughters

of the witch
who would not burn

iii

it's a complication,
a major complication:

you lot always asking us:

when was it that you knew

when did you know
the world would be different,

that it was not the same for you

it when your brother had no chores,
while you helped with laundry,
and the food,

or when you started school, and
weren't allowed
to wear shorts,
n play that footy,

what was the moment,

you realised
you were a girl

a complication, in b major

is you

never registering
black girls' silence,
our confusion

it is not a possibility
to you that
some of us
never get
to learn

we know
from get-go

a bigger complication, a
braver complication, a
blacker complication

looms

unholy alliance

they arrive
at the meeting
all grouped together:

an old, familiar hatred

flickering

in their eyes

waving, and
walking confidently over,
they stab their right hands
across the colour divide

as if, of course,
    we black women

have been waiting
        for this
unholy alliance

all our live-long lives

they say:

sisters,
now sisters,

ain't we all women,
we don't see colour,
and *those days are long gone*

let us stand together,
against the ones arriving:

their children do not belong
in our schools

they must not touch
        the drinking fountains

and then,

there's the matter

of the bathrooms

ariel

after sylvia plath

that word,

slap in the centre
of sylvia's
'ariel'

slur, on the darkness
of poets like me

and oh, they drum us
towards the altar
          of lazarus

but our wick

remains
          un-lit

whispers

her son was friends
          with mine

in first grade,
at the local primary school

or perhaps, they were more
acquaintances
(the two were
always falling out,
and of course i never said,
but i was pretty sure
whose fault that was)

i just think it's so sad,
you splitting up,

                    she said,
          you know,
it ruins the lives
of the kids

in cartoon rendition,
her nose would have been
triangularly up-pointed

the kids are perfectly
                    happy,

i assured

then mused:
and maybe

'unhappy'
is being trapped
in a home

where the folks
who made you

no longer love
each other,

and you're
subliminally aware

they're faking it
for your benefit

mute rage
flushed her drawn-in cheeks:
veritable capillaries
of outrage, and scorn

i recounted her reaction
to my mother, that evening

there's a saying guyanese
folk have,
mum said:
'some people are not happy
unless you are as unhappy
as they are'

next morning,
the row of mothers
outside at drop-off
wouldn't look
          in my direction,
as if *leaving* were contagious

selfish
          someone muttered,
under their breath

i heard the school mum
whose son was
always falling out with mine

moved back to adelaide
the very next year

she took the kids,
and he took the house:

shacked up
with a woman
from work

#IWD Lament

and though we all
          would like
to thank you,
for humouring us,
on this special day,

we also need you
          to stop killing us,
the dishes done,

and equal pay

VIOLAZIONE

violazione

silver nonno, shuffling past
in the late morning sun,

halts, at the gate
of my suburban front garden

i look up,
from the veggie bed
i'm assembling

and he takes my smile
as an invitation

the old man

wanders in;
turns a slow lap
of the shiny cherry tomatoes;
          rubs a leaf of
a flourishing basil bush
between thumb and fore;
picks a sprig of oregano,
          and sniffs;

bends, creakily, to pull
a pak carrot from the soil

i watch him,
silent with disbelief

on completing his tour,
nonno nods in approval,
and swivels his eyes
in my direction,

taking in
        the spanner in my hand,
and the last incomplete panel
of the enormous steel
birdie i'm building

don't you have a husband
who can do that for you

he says

but it isn't
a question

i tighten the last bolt,
    and straighten up,

tilt my face
to the late summer glare

good morning
i hope you've enjoyed my vegetables

now get the fuck off my lawn

what het men don't want

a woman taller than them
a woman darker than them
a woman smarter than them
who earns more

a woman with children
a woman who can't have children
a woman who doesn't want children
        or wants more

a woman who speaks her mind
a woman who knows her own mind
a woman who just can't make up her mind
    an unfit woman
a woman too fat
a bony woman

too fit
or too strong

a woman who's happy
a miserable woman
a woman who's always depressed

an 'overconfident' woman
a capable woman
a woman with low self-esteem

a woman who needs no one
a 'needy' woman
a woman who 'just won't leave them alone'

a feeding woman
or a bleeding woman
a woman who's not a walking womb

a woman who's ripped
or a woman who's stitched
or a woman who can't *give birth vaginally*

a scarred woman
or a scared woman
or a woman not scared of a thing

a woman who 'smothers' them
a loyal woman
a dedicated woman
a woman aloof

a tentative woman
a careless woman
a woman who is 'too hard to please'

a natural woman
a plastic woman
a made-up woman
or a woman who's 'plain'

a real woman
a catfish

a woman they know,
or a woman who they don't

the ninth sense

the young couple
in front
at the bakery store
          his hand casual
on the back of her neck:

thumb to the right side,
fingers curved round the left,

the way she tilts away,
          just gently

woman pacing the bus stop,
shoes still in hand,
shaking, but saying she's *fine*,

looking over her shoulder
as the bus pulls away,

          then, her sigh
as we round the corner

the friend at work,
who says she's
no good with money:
doesn't even know
what they own

but i kind of like
that he deals with those things

fingernails chewed:
down to the quick

every nine days,
a woman is murdered
by someone she loves,

or once loved

but at the bus stop, in the bakery
and in the coffee break room

they are living, today,

amongst us

disordered glossary

a bit of alright
adorable
always a bridesmaid (never a bride)

angry black woman
asking for it
attention seeker
babe

baby mama
barren
battleaxe
batty

biddy
bimbo
bitter
bitch
bit-on-the-side
bitchy

black widow
blossoming
bombshell

bossy

broody
bubbly
buzzkill

career woman
cat lady
cheap
chick
clucky
clothes horse
cougar
crone
cute
dainty
daddy's-little-girl
damaged goods
damsel in distress

dance mum
darling
diva
dear

debbie downer
deflowered

delicate
demure
dish
ditzy
does-the-carpet-match-the-drapes

dragon lady
drama queen
dried-up
doll

don't-worry-your-pretty-little-head-about-that

doormat
dotty
easy
fat chick
feisty
feminine charm

femme fatale

flibbertigibbet
flirt
flirty
floozy
frigid
girlfriend material

girly
gold-digger
good girl

grandmotherly
hag

happy wife, happy life

harlot
harpy
having it all
ho

homewrecker
honey

honeytrap
housewife
hussy
hysterical

ice queen

jailbait
jezebel

kept woman
knocked up
little lady
ladylike

lady in the streets, freak in the sheets
lady of the night

left on the shelf
loopy
loose
love
man-hater
maternal

matronly
mistress
mother hen
motherfucker
mothering instinct

mousy
mummy blogger
mumpreneur
mumsy
mutton-dressed-as-lamb

nasty
nesting
nice nelly
not like the other girls

old bat
other woman
overbearing
overconfident
oversensitive
plus size

pop-the-cherry
pretty-when-you-smile
precocious
prima donna
princess

sassy
scrag
sheila

shotgun wedding
she-wolf
shrew

shrieking
shrill
sidepiece

sissy
skirt
slip-of-a-thing

slut
slutty

starfish

soccer mum
spinster
spring chicken

squealing like a banshee

sweetie
sweetheart

tease
tomboy
town bike
trollop

trophy wife
unladylike
used goods
vixen
wallflower

watching her figure
wearing the pants

wench
whore
wife material

witch
working girl
working mother

work wife

the bear wants dinner

about twenty-five years
        into the new century
a kolkotan trainee doctor
was raped and murdered,

as she napped
between shifts

meanwhile,
    upside the world,

madame gisèle pelicot
discovered her own husband

had been drugging her,
        for years:
offering her to willing men,
in the quaint french village
where they lived

and so, twenty-five years
into the new century,
we women started saying:

i choose the bear

would rather take my chances
with two hundred and seventy kilos

of carnivorous,
          snarling

animal,

than the beast
man surely is

the bear will not roll back legislation,
to mandate we give birth
to our rapist's child

the bear will not set fire
to our very souls, and stand over us,
with an odd, lopsided smile,

as flame makes crackling
of our tender skin

the bear will not sniff the air
—heavy with the meat
of our burning—
watch our agony,

          and laugh

the bear just seeks
to feed its children

the bear
wants
dinner,

and that is all

reasonable doubt

is this a photo
of what you were wearing
,but did you say—

no?

and how much
had you had to—

drink!

you and he'd had sex before?!

so what was it that made this time
'wrong'
,at least, in your opinion

and you went back to his place
,that's right?
(some would say that was *teasing*)
—withdrawn!

(i mean, what did you think
you were there for)
—withdrawn!

(a cup of tea and a biscuit?)
    —withdrawn!

we submit
that it was
    consensual, miss

,and, perhaps,
you had regrets
in the morning

can you really remember?

    really, i mean?

you'd had quite a bit to—
    just think!

,come on,
did he *really* undress you,

or was it
    you,

who undressed

him?

honk

eat alone

order seconds,
while reading a book

then wipe your hands
on your shirt

shave your head,
love the way it looks

when it grows out,
do it again

on work photo day,
wear a bright orange suit—
or just gadding
about the house

say *what the fuck*
are you looking at

laugh loudly: in the office,
and on the tram

swear
and if they stare,
then swear again

wear no bra
when you pop to the shops

don't pop to the shops

never wear a bra

honk at men
who cut you off

on the road,
or, y'know, just casually,

in conversations,

in real life

honk,
and keep on honking

go on
for as long

as you like

TO HAVE BECOME

to have become

to have become
the woman
i'd have stood
in awe of,

if ever i'd known
that woman
could be

that, alone,
is enough

for me

grown

nineteen, and assured,

he stands by the stove,
stirring the spaghetti sauce, talking:

how late his shift ran last night; how
one of his lecturers *just irks him*
this semester; the amazing theatre tickets
he just got for free;

how he never knew, not
till this very moment,

that celery was the secret
ingredient, in my most
frequently rotated dish

a grown-now man,
my god

think of it:

after the joy, and
the shit, and the bliss,
and the funk, and
the sheer, overwhelming
          wrestle of it

a grown-now man

who still slams
the front door

a little too hard
on arrival home

as if to yell,

in that brash,
school-afternoon way:

mama! mama!
i'm home!

the entire goddamn
height of him; the
three-day stubble;

the final squaring
of post-teen chin

cause no one places
that shiny newborn
          into your arms
in the delivery room, and says

well, congratulations,
you made a man,

but here one is:

clumsy, and funny,
and delightful, and smart,

but not too big to be told

to speak
          just a little more quietly,

and leave

just

a little

more room

woke

shine, like a beacon;
remain alert

do not be afraid
of flushing the shadows

remember,

they want you
asleep on their watch

collaboration

you'll have your place,
          and i'll have mine,
and we won't worry
that it isn't real

we won't complete each other,
but we'll love each other,

we'll understand
how great that is

sometimes we'll sleep
side by side for weeks,

          and some months,
we'll sleep alone

or i won't answer calls for days,
and you'll swing by my home,

and i'll be scrawling poems
at my kitchen table: stray pages
strewn on every surface,

writing in marker,

on the mirrors,

and you'll be relieved,
        but won't be hurt,

so early mornings you'll sneak in,
and fill my fridge, and do the dishes,

and you'll brew the coffee strong,

and next month,
i'll do the same for you

and if we're both at work,
        we'll eat out together,
heads bowed, scribbling on unlined paper:
silent, absorbed, and rude to watch,
then we'll retire to our own places

and damn, we'll love this life

we will adore this life:

rich, uncompromised,
and of our making

there'll be cheese on toast,
and fancy dinners,
and catching up with the kids

who you've known and loved
        most their lives,
and who have grown
into brilliant humans

we might sign up for foster respite,
if we can spare
        the time and love,

or we'll entertain the grands on saturdays,
or school-day afternoons—

or not

maybe at your place, you'll have a dog,
        and i'll just learn to fucking cope,
(or, likely, swear under my breath,
as you laugh, and it licks my shoes)

and we'll travel,
and we'll walk the galleries,
and i'll garden,
        if still inclined

you'll cut glowing bunches
of my marigolds, borage,
and nasturtium

that we'll display in matching vases
to show off to our friends

as we throw dinner parties,
at yours or mine,
        or even in the street

we'll make simple food:

maybe unearthed
from my jungled veggie beds

i will cook,
and you will clean,

and we'll laugh long
into the evening:
with artists, nurses, and the teachers,
circus folk, and
the dreamers

and when the money's gone,
we'll plot the next

great

collaboration

you'll have your place,
and i'll have mine,

and we will be
each other's places

untouchable

i am untouchable:

a dangerous example
for their growing girls

a woman, successful,
and complete,

in the company
of herself

casual revolution

in the quiet fleetings

ear to the cotton,
finally succumbing
to the ink-blue hours
of a love-long writing night

i marvel, at this
casual revolution

this woman, dark,
and furious:

marking the rhythms
of deep naarm winter

at the boatwood kitchen table

spinning poems into groceries,
and poems into rent money, and prose
into clothes, gas, electric,
and school fees

while her children,

who think this
an ordinary life,

turn lightly,

in their dreams

good enough

just news
of your impending arrival,
my darling,

adjusted everything
in the world

the sonographer smiled
at the scattered white dots,

and your brother
pumped his tiny fist

right from that *girl* moment,
my heart was asking
at every turn, and
as sure as i breathed:

would i want this
for my daughter,

and if not,

why on earth
should it be
good enough

for me

The Hope of a Thousand Small Lights

for the women who fought for the equality of the International Criminal Court, and those who warrior on

i. The Task

Joy, for many,

it is made up
of the simple wonders of this life.

Sometimes we do not know it,
and it's only at the end
we can recall
the feeling
of a tiny hand in ours:

cherubic face upturned,
wide-eyed with trust,

as we remind a young one
where to cross
    the road,
    their t's,
    a stitch they dropped,
    their plastic knitting needles,

fingers, when they tell a fib,
and oh,
their tiny hearts

(which one day
we all know will break
over somebody
or some thing
that matters most).

The simple wonders of this life:
oh, innocence,
and women
walking arm in arm
on quiet dusk-descended streets,
in safety:
laughter singing sisterhood.

Delightful in their whimsy.
Stunning in their calm ferocity.
At ease, and glorious,
in casual and unthinking freedom.

Joy is the tiny wonders of this life,

bequeathed so readily to some:
a meal with friends;
shelter on icy nights;
family together;
dignity and hearth;
a tender body,
loving unconditionally when winter falls.

The space and strength to say:
this life is mine,
this right is mine,
this body's mine,
this choice is mine,
this thought is mine,
and mine alone.

The simple wonders of this life,
and of these rights:
profound-unearned.
Intrinsic and inalienable.

Not to be sold,
or spent,
or spared.

Not to be spat at,
spurned or savaged.

That's the task.

That *is* the task:
to light up
the darkened corners
where these joys have been denied.

To strike the match
that lights the lamp.
And heavens, what an ask:
to flood with brightness,
and to search the shadows
where the worst of our humanity has gathered.

To square up against
the sure-unspeakable, and say:
    Enough!
    This cannot be what we're made of.
    This cannot be what we sleep on.
    This cannot be what we let to breed,

and rot, and fester.

Oh, the horrors
found marauding in the margins
where the many do not tread.

That is the task:
to lay a hand on trauma's shoulder,
turn it round, and
look it in the eye.

To say:
this must be brought to justice:
we are searching,
we are watching.
We will find you—
when we find you,
we will never look away.

To acknowledge
that there walk amongst us reapers:
scythes at the ready,
riding the horses of war and mayhem,
slaying all that we hold dear.

Sniffing the air
    for the scent
of those so vulnerable
they cannot—dare not—
raise:
    their fists to fight,
    their voices-loud,
    objections,
    international alarm.

Yes, this is what was realised
that summer, there,
in the city of seven hills.

Oh, this is
what was born,
in Rome,

at the conception
of the International Criminal Court.

A vow, by seal of nations,
resolute-united,
saying:

we will chase the shadows
to the round, unending edges
of this aching earth.
No matter famine, war or fire,
fall of state or flood.

No matter dissidence
or disobedience,
or tragedy, or ruin.

Life itself
is sacred.

There are acts
which chill the blood.

And we will, together,
will, we swear,

protect those folks

the greatest darkness
finds.

ii. The Mandate

Some say the law
ought not to bend.

That it should be a neutral,
certain thing.

But there are reasons
judgement and interpretation
are bequeathed
to human
—humane—
hearts and heads.

Enter women, in coalition:

women, from the wings
of all the world,

who raised the plight
of territories

from the Balkans to Rwanda.

From fields of conflict,
    and beyond.

These women urged the court
to recognise that category of crimes
which, by the horror of their calculation,
    target women

—target women, and their daughters
by the tent there, playing catch;

target women, and the sleeping children
strapped to buckling backs;

target women, and their cheeky nephews,
dirt-drawing twig-in-hand;

target women, and the crawling babes, look,
right by their feet—

and the crimes which target
those whom gender,
(in the minds
of misogynistic men

and their supporters),

make
        as vulnerable
as these.

There are some crimes
which, by design,
so make of man
the enemies of all mankind.

So the sisterhood
walked the corridors of power:
lobbied, whispered, woke
and wrangled
in the halls of Rome.

The sisterhood
stole little sleep,
and guided by the soul
of some other-worldly strength,
—and bleary-eyed,
and sure of heart,

worked tirelessly

to see the statute recognise
the folk the greatest horrors

always find.

Whatever you do to the least of my sisters.
Every woman is a sister of mine.

And where war walks,
its bed-friend torture lounges,

to test the very limits
of what a broken body
                    can bear.

For those whom gender makes a mark of
when the world forgets to watch,

for them,

the women guarding the statute of Rome,
they coalesced, they did their best

to weave through law
an equal gaze.

To see that women always walk the halls,
and sit the benches:
see that there is always pause

to think of what it means
to be a woman in this world.

And to encourage those there judging
to bring to table, and to thinking,
all their living's taught them
(and perhaps the very things their living's
taught them are unimportant).

And oh, they were at pains to see
that academic theorisation

would not prove the enemy
of *just* interpretation.

And so it was the court,
there writ through treaty,

realised, and recognised
and ratified

a place,

the space,

for Feminist
consideration.

When, much later,
warm, fresh from the press,
the thing was set to paper,
they had achieved

not all their aims
(and many, true, lamented
that the pull of status quo
stripped back the goals
of progress).

But, still,

that they so tried,
and would not give in,
that they *believed*,

that was enough

to embed
a gender mandate
in the ICC.

When all was said and done,
and when dawn broke in Rome,
there bled a sunrise, peach and golden,
flecked with dappled rose,
that faded out
into the morning blue.

A glimmer of hope
that change would come.

Something had shifted,
everyone knew.

iii. The Measure

When the stench of terror
still hangs in the air,

and the slain
are yet to be given their rites;

when the shelling has stopped,
but the copters still whirr
in near, not distant, memory.

When children crawl, trembling,
from out of their cupboards,

eyes terror-wide,
and darting.

When word finally spreads
that it's safe on the ground
and the task begins,
          of searching.

When mourning arrives,

and the wailing continues;

with the damage surveyed,
and the losses inventoried.

When the shock sets in,
and the shaking commences,

and husbands crawl forward
to cradle their wives.

What the measure of justice, then:
what the measure of success.

What of the vow of '98:

the united hands
which would drive back hatred
and brutality; inhumanity, and fear.

What of the court built to raise survivors
—to raise their stories to the sky:

what of their brave whispers,
            and their justice-cry.

What of this court
that was built to give pause
for interpreters to speak,
with supports at the ready,
and *ready to hear*

the facts, unfettered,
and ferocious,
—*ferocious*, in their telling.

Built on the edge
of the northern sea,
deep in The Hague,
in the City of Peace:

Saltwater to truth.
An oceanic breeze.

Oh, let the light in,

let the light in,

to dance through the darkened halls.

To pirouette and tumble,
and to search out every shadow:

refracting,
and reflecting,
and unfiltered,
and aglow.

Brilliant women
were nominated to the bench:
in numbers justice,
and her sisters, favoured.
Women of all axes,
persuasion, and thought
(there were some triumphs, after all).

But in crept the corners
of status quo.

Unprecedent thrived,

and unwieldy process:

Certain crimes
weren't recognised
as particular
        in their horror:

    the plight of girl soldiers,
and their bodies as tools,
and their freedom denied,
and their labour subsumed,

and war commanders were shielded
    by the chain of command,

and women forced to bear children
    had justice denied,

and they dismissed crimes designed
to de-masculinise
                and desexualise boys and men.

And the experts were challenged,
and testimony decried,

and stigma stayed tongues,
and the States closed their eyes.

The corners of status quo crept in,
to restrict the justice there *could* have been

if what happened in Rome
hadn't stayed in Rome,

and the mandate
was followed through—

and the court had stood proud,
and bared all its teeth,

to do
what it was *born*
          to do.

iv. The Map

What use the pen,
if not to protect.

What remedy ink,
if not a salve,

and what use reason,
if not to reason *well.*

What of a mandate for reform
without the *courage* to reform,

What becomes of a revolution
that doubts *itself.*

Well, now takes hold,
across the globe,
an epic reimagining:

a movement, whispering
across the wide-deep oceans.

A radical unpicking
of the neat, and patriarchal, stitch

embedded in the fabric
of unwieldy man-made law.

For what wonder is critique,
if condemnation's withheld.

If the judgements are untouchable; revered.

And so, the many pens
of Feminist thought,

in deep and honest contemplation,

bleed ink for the judgements
there might have been:

if bravery,
and courage
and equality
    and reform
had turned the corner of The Hague
and stared down, proper, face-to-face,

the casual-unthinking bias
of international criminal law.

Law made *by* men,

and made *for* men,
which makes *of* men
the perfect injured;

makes of men defendants,
judges, sentencers, and all.

For some, the law's lean
cannot be unwritten

(through process, judge
or survivor's hearing),

for at its foundation there is rot,
and colonial conquer, and imposition.

But critique will cartograph the map:
myriad voices, in good faith and fact.

Let another scholar now spark their lamp,
and unwrite into the night.

And in the darkness, *there*, it flickers:
the hope of a thousand small lights.

As another,
and another,
and another,

unwrites,

and the harmony
of choral-collective
          takes flight.

As Feminist scholars
of all genders and creeds

light up the darkened corners
where world justice has been denied.

We will strike the match
that glows the lamp.
And heavens, what an ask.

Oh, *change.*
Oh, women
—and their allies—
writing desk by desk

on quiet dusk-descending nights:
in starts, with distant gunfire,
tired, resolute, or charged,

their labour singing sisterhood,

at ease, and glorious,

in sure, and fierce, and conscious

freedom.

men, in the effort

men moving, men marching,
men walking with purpose,
men spilling into laneways,
men, swarming the earth,
men chanting, men calling,
waving signs from the windows,
men sighing, men sobbing,
testifying grown men, oh
just men, yeah, just men,
just men, in their millions,
pounding the pavements
with placarded opinions

men lobbying,
men petitioning,
men white/purple ribboning
male allies, male good guys,
as-a-husbands,
pink ribbons,

cause-of-sister men,
love-mister men,
and men for-no-reason

other than knowing
that women
        deserve freedom

right-to-choose men
in jimmy choos, men:
flamboyant, and fucking fabulous,
fighting for the rights
of the woman who carried them

protecting the lives
        of the women they love

men standing,
men marching,
for the one
        who loves them

motivated men, slack men,
woke but privileged-as-all-that men
small men, and fat men,
just calling all men

men off the couch,
men who'll vouch,
        men who'll say what they've seen
and men who'll stop mates
from doing the wrong thing,

male friends,
and male enemies,
male ceos and employees

male allies, male all-eyes,
men ready to defend against
offender men

feminist men

calling all men

status-quo-must-end men,
and on-message tender men,
poets, and tradies,
and stay-at-home-dads

fist-in-the-fight men
and shy-but-alright men

men, in the effort,
with whatever they can bring:

chocolate, or childcare,
proximity to power

silence or promotion,
legislation, or bail

men lining up
to log what they'll offer
on upcycled clipboards
that are handmade by men

with apologies and apostrophes,
and sign-making skills,
with sewing machines, cranes,
and hundred-dollar bills

with the town plans,
and tractors,
and bulletproof vests

men, in their millions,
all saying: *we're in*

THE MATRIARCHS

tribute

my great-grandma
        lay down
at thirty-eight

nan passed
at fifty-nine

my mum, bold-vibrant,
        in her seventies now

each generation
of fierce black women

pays tribute

by staying alive

alice, alone

auburn light
in the authors lounge

and here she is:
alice, alone

looking just as much my aunty,
as the legend alice walker,
if that's not sacrilege to say

i don't remember
walking towards her,

but suddenly, here i am:
throat making strange, dry, airy sounds

where i know there should be words

my soul
has been stunned

by the gravity
of this moment,

and then, suddenly,

she's gone

haiku

she invites herself,
when i don't pick up the phone
brings coffee: cold brew

dishes fill my sink;
the floors sticky, unvacuumed
she rolls up her sleeves

to fill the silence,
she gossips, jokes and skylarks,
dish foam on her chin

when the work is done,
we stare out at the garden:
my voice, a surprise

saving grace

the teller
        sat straight-backed
behind the bank counter,
long brown hair
slicked into
official-looking ponytail

my partner and i
had our first child in tow:

a charming toddler
partial to poached eggs,
smiling unabashedly at strangers,
and vegemite toast,

  he made straight
for the busy intersection

beyond the commbank
sliding doors,

and his father stepped away
to chase him,

in that tiny glimpse
of a moment,

the teller
          leaned over,
fast, and deliberate,

branded name brooch
catching on the black
plastic counter,

and whispered:
          one signature,
          or two?

i stared back quizzically

she repeated, more hurriedly,
eyes fixed on my
returning family

          one signature,
          or two?

with one signature,
you can get the money out
from a joint savings account
by yourself

clearing her throat,
meaningfully

one, please

i snatched the words
from the back of my throat:
my voice low, and unfamiliar

my little family returned,

and she hit a key on her computer,
smiling friendly up
at my wriggling son

you're a boisterous one!

handing over
the printed paperwork, then:
rightio, folks,
that's all done!

there was never
any violence,

but four years later,
when i left,
with two babes in tow,

i quietly used
my single signature

to withdraw half
our hopes

the homemakers

in sodden sleeping bags
beneath bridges;

in sheltered nooks
of shuttered shops;

weary at the windows
of mobile kitchens
women, homeless,
in their dusk

fingers thawing
on paper cups

tucked in lined hands
by hopeful volunteers

with no time
          for life stories,
lingering,
a second serve,
or tears

there's another corner
they've got to serve
another cup, another blanket,
more bread—

the wind tonight
is vicious, you find
a shelter now, you hear

dusk-women
cracked lips,
blistered fingers;
bruised hearts, histories,
        and minds

battered souls,
finances, trust, and bodies,
confidence,
        and thoughts

dusk,

and pushing fifty,
pushing sixty, pushing
trolleys, pushing all
they own

women,

who for so very long,

and for everyone
who knocked, or needed,

        smiled,
got out another plate,
grabbed the spare sheets,

and made room

bound

for Kath

can you bring the kids

they might want
to say goodbye
        to their grandmother

the hospital says
there's not much time

it was as near to death
as i had ever been:
stiff hospital sheets
smoothed so flat, it seemed
she'd already left the room

her fingers translucent:
you could see the joints,
see through to bone

this loud,
        intellectual giant

of an irishblood

was slipping

          into quiet

she opened her eyes,
just for a moment,

and beneath the ivory
shock of fringe,
she smiled,
and said, barely audible,
          to the nurses

this is my daughter-in-law

in that moment
i realised,

though there was no marriage,
        and her son and i
had now been apart
for much longer
than we were together,

and though now,
there was also another

she'd never stopped
calling me that:

my daughter-in-law

even here,
so close to the end,
thin tallow fingers
clasped lovingly

around my eldest's
        gentle brown hand,

she was making
an effort to say:

life bound us
together, so unexpectedly

but oh,

how glad i am

for the matriarchs

thank you,
joyous marching aunties
butch, in mardi gras silver suits:
flipping us off, calling us out,
        holding us fucking accountable

nans with empty cupboards,
but a talent for anchor stitch,
turning a seam for any folk
        who find their sewing room

that public school teacher,
with an extra lunchbox, and a lucky dip of dreams
who keeps the door open during breaks,
        and always eats alone

the social worker who understands
rules are there to protect *and* bend,
that sometimes the thing for a fighting child
        is to sleep in their own bed

midwives, who'll coax mums to their feet,
whispering *gravity's gracious*—

who'll buy time to stall the doctor
from a needless operation

ceo, who cracked the ceiling,
stashing the sledgehammer by her side:
pulling through those who come up after,
standing sentinel-alert

thank you, glamourous giving trans queens
who gather young lost souls
the world has tarred as aberration—
humming, *welcome, you are home*

and designers who make garments
for a genuine big gal's stride
(cut to hips, wings, folds and fupas,
and not just an upscaled five)

thanks, banner makers, and risk-takers,
protesters and the kweens,
bakers and the homemakers,
bosses, bitches, and the dreamers,

the sisters, and the mamas
and the aunties-of-them-all,

the makers and the movers,
sex workers, gynos, and the nuns

my mother, my sister, my daughter
and yours, and hers, and theirs

thank you,

matriarchs-in-the-making,
and matriarchs,

        on your thrones

EPILOGUE

the ones who return

when my mother leaves
for the grocery store,

i put the baby down
          in another room
and curl up
on my childhood bed

i sleep desperately,
     but with vigilance,

as all new mothers do:

am fully weighted
into the darkness,
          when i hear

the old wooden rocking chair
in the corner of the living room,
start a slow, and rhythmic,
                                        creaking

i ease myself up,
and shuffle

towards the sound:
down the corridor,
past my sister's old room; past
my brother's, too

my mother's mother,
        long gone now,

sits in the rocking chair,
        head bowed,

wearing the same camel-coloured suit
and pink-flowered hat
she has on
        in the photo
that sits on the out-of-tune piano

immediately i know:
she is wearing that get-up
so i recognise her,

she does not want me
    to be alarmed

as i advance,
i notice
her arms are full:
a swaddled, squirming,
light blue cocoon

with loose black curls
          poking through

nana mildred
cradles her great-grandbaby
in her arms,

and smiles,
and rocks, and coos

and smiles,
and rocks, and coos

i only saw my nana's spirit
that one time

and i am not religious
        about a thing

but it makes sense, y'know,

that the women of our family
would barter, and borrow,
and bargain, and argue,
and beg

do anything they could
in this world, or the next,

to be sure

they could welcome

        their kin

ACKNOWLEDGEMENTS

beautiful changelings was written on the land of the Wurundjeri, Woi Wurrung and Boonwurrung People of the Kulin Nation, where I live and work – on land that always was, and always will be, Aboriginal land. I am grateful for the stories and storytellers that have kept this place, since time immemorial, and for the opportunity to live and create in this extraordinary place.

My publishing story began many years ago, at the microphone. Thank you to the poets who were there at the beginning of it all, sharing poems and stages, triumphs and edits at *The Dan O'Connell*, *The Spinning Room*, *Queensland Poetry Festival*, *Overload Poetry Festival*, *Melbourne Spoken Word and Poetry Festival*, *The Believer Slam*, *Passionate Tongues*, *Poetry Idol*, *Liner Notes*, and all the other playgrounds in which we poetically postured. Your ears, your cheers, your finger clicks, your support, your notes, your critiques, and your camaraderie sing within me, still.

Thanks to those who've supported me to do what I do over the years by assisting with childcare, teen hangs, and/or enduring the occasional (or not so occasional) frustrated rant about creative life, the writing industry, the mental load, the financial load, and so on, and so forth: including Monique Hameed, Claudette Clarke, Lian Low, Silvano Giordano, Murray Nance, Jinghua Qian, Raina Peterson, Liz Shield, Ann Dinh, and Kate and Robbie Hendry.

I extend my unwavering gratitude to those who've programmed, pushed, awarded, and amplified my work over the years, including Susan Armstrong, David Stavanger, Anne-Marie Te Whiu, Rob Riel, Jeff Sparrow, Erik Jensen, Michael Nolan, Alicia Sometimes, Emilie Zoey Baker, Samah Sabawi, Marieke Hardy, Veronica Sullivan, David Ryding, Sam Twyford-Moore, Francesca Rendle-Short, Paddy O'Reilly, Kate Larsen, Lisa Dempster, Anthony O'Sullivan, Steve Smart, Amanda Anastasi, Di Cousens, Michael Reynolds, and Deb Force.

To the poets with whom I had conversations about poetry and words while working on *beautiful changelings*, not necessarily about this work, but which nonetheless invigorated my love for the form, and urged me to push on, including Nadia Niaz, Magan Magan, Srishti Chatterji, and Maria van Neerven – thank you.

The poem *women's work* was commissioned by the Victorian Women's Trust and was first published in 2021.

The poem *The Hope of a Thousand Small Lights* was first published in *Feminist Judgements: Reimagining the International Criminal Court* (Cambridge University Press, 2025), edited by Kcasey McLoughlin, Rosemary Grey, Louise Chappell, and Suzanne Varrall. Thank you, in particular, to Professor Louise Chappell of the Australian Human Rights Institute at UNSW Sydney, and to Associate Professor Kcasey McLoughlin of The University of Newcastle, for their ongoing support of my work, and their profound understanding of the intersections between poetry and the law.

A previous version of the poem *possum magic* was first written for (and performed at) The Wheeler Centre's *Mum's the World Gala* in 2023.

The poem *boxing day* was previously published in my poetry chapbook *nothing here needs fixing* (2013).

An earlier version of poem *spindle* was first published as a numbered, signed limited edition zine, as part of the zine swap at The University of Melbourne's *Encounters with Writing* student writing festival in 2024, during my time as Poet in Residence (hold on to those zines students, they just might be worth something some day!).

Thanks to my daughter and her school friends, for being the story behind the poem *a good wait*. I am Mum-taxi for life now, to a chorus of 'But we inspire you!'

A heartfelt thank you to Dr Fiona Reilly and Dr Mariam Tokhi, for inviting me to be part of the change, teaching in their groundbreaking *Narrative Medicine* course at The University of Melbourne, and to the three cohorts of medical students I've now taught in this space. Without this experience, and the poignant conversations with young medical professionals in this course, I doubt I'd have had the courage to include the narrative poem *i would like a hysterectomy* in this collection. The work you are all doing is difficult, honest, and vital – it gives me hope for a world in which no person has to fear seeking medical assistance.

Thank you to the extraordinary team at Ultimo Press. Thanks to Robert Watkins – at first my publisher, but over the years, a dear, dear friend. Thank you publicist extraordinaire Zoë Victoria, for your fierce championing of my work, thanks editor Sophie Mayfield for your patience and eagle eye, and Andrea Johnson, the marketing guru. Thank you, once again, to editor Ali Lavau, *who sees all the things*, and to illustrator and designer Allison Colpoys, for the phenomenally beautiful cover. Thank you Elena Gomez, for the proofread, and Leah Jing McIntosh, for the author photo.

Thank you, thank you, *thank you.*

A book is not just the sum of the author's thoughts and efforts, but of all the hands and hearts that held the author and ushered the book on its way.

Last but not least, thank you to my extended family, for their ongoing support as I wade through these volatile creative waters: including Claudette, Syreeta, Braden, Mali, Maya, Ayana, Jasmine – and, of course, to Ernest.

PHOTO: LEAH JING McINTOSH

Maxine Beneba Clarke is one of Australia's most celebrated poets. She is the author of over fourteen books, including the bestselling memoir *The Hate Race*, the ABIA and Indie award-winning short fiction collection *Foreign Soil*, the Victorian Premier's Award-winning poetry collection *Carrying the World*, the ABIA award-winning poetry collection *It's the Sound of the Thing*, the Kate Greenaway Medal longlisted illustrated poem *When We Say Black Lives Matter* and the CBCA honour book *The Patchwork Bike*, which also won the Boston Globe Horn Prize for Best Picture Book. She was the inaugural Peter Steele Poet in Residence at The University of Melbourne.